Of Thee I Sing

The University of Georgia Press

Athens and London

OF THEE
I SING

Poems by

Timothy Liu

Published by the University of Georgia Press
Athens, Georgia 30602
© 2004 by Timothy Liu
All rights reserved
Designed by Mindy Basinger Hill
Set in 11/14 Centaur
Printed and bound by Thomson-Shore
The paper in this book meets the guidelines for permanence
and durability of the Committee on Production Guidelines
for Book Longevity of the Council on Library Resources.

Printed in the United States of America

08   07   06   05   04   P   5   4   3   2   1

Library of Congress Cataloging-in-Publication Data

Liu, Timothy.
Of thee I sing : poems / by Timothy Liu.
p. cm.
ISBN 0-8203-2600-3 (pbk. : alk. paper)
I. Asian American gays—Poetry. 2. Gay men—Poetry. I. Title.
PS3562.I799O36 2004
811'.54—dc22

2003019204

British Library Cataloging-in-Publication Data available

Contents

Acknowledgments

Many thanks to the editors of the following publications in which these poems first appeared: *Black Warrior Review, Chelsea, Columbia: A Journal of Literature and Art, Cortland Review, Crab Orchard Review, Denver Quarterly, FIELD, Gettysburg Review, Global City Review, Heart Quarterly, Indiana Review, Interim, Iowa Review, The Journal, Kenyon Review, Luna, Massachusetts Review, Mid-American Review, Missouri Review, The Nation, North American Review, Paris Review, Perihelion, Phoebe, Pleiades, Ploughshares, Poetry East, The Quarterly, Quarterly West, Ribot, River Styx, Skanky Possum, Slope, Sonora Review, Southeast Review, Tin House, Verse, Washington Square,* and *Yale Review.*

"Felix Culpa" was reprinted in *The Best American Poetry* 2002, edited by Robert Creeley (Scribners, 2002).

"F-Stop," "From Sea to Shining Sea," "Il Trittico," "Triptych in Black Lipstick," and "Waking Up" were reprinted in the chapbook *A Mighty Fortress* (Thorngate Road, 2001).

For friends tried and true, I thank Bruce Beasley, Christopher Davis, and Christine Hume for their necessary company during the writing of this book.

"Sweet land of liberty . . ."

I

Ars Poetica

Even then those fissures could be seen.

Once a grand hotel in another age.

Yes it was, wasn't it, he said.

All the world day-trading suicide shares.

Sinking through the valves of sleep.

Crowned by spurts of milky jet.

The craft could be taught but not the art.

Duck Hunting

Kokoschka's woman mostly wound, left
to fend for herself in a bathing suit under
pastel skies—eyes fixed on that mallard
driven down. A dog among the reeds
afloat on his own shadow—bestial gaze
malingering on a female form who stands
in a flesh canoe. No other signs of life
to hold our attention, only an abandoned
cottage at the picture's edge, the hunter
kept from view. This work's all muscled
torque where canine shoulders dissolve
to strokes of blue—a gun-shaped smudge
of the artist's blood angled in the scrub.

GIACOMETTI

The work of his hands cannot cry.
The mouths that cannot breathe
or speak took hours to make.
Beauty was not required. Only
hands that spoke two languages.
All it took to make a human cry.

Triptych in Black Lipstick

I. Image

Decor we want to trash as we get more
sloshed on sangria. My cocktail
fork clatters to the floor, and I ask
to be excused. Who else could love
that woman trapped inside my bones?—
blackened lips blowing on a toilet-
paper veil, the stall's steel plate
pried back. Was it cruising underneath
gothic arches that made us horny?—
Caravaggio's mannerist eye nothing
more than an axis of descent: Christ's
halo floodlit by the body's eternal
chiaroscuro until an angel rolls away
the stone. Wing's tip. The buttocks
of a man hunched over where strangers
kneel before a row of marble urinals—
no talk, only grunts behind a door
where we watch ourselves get blown
in the mirror. I return to find you
bloodshot on a bar stool, mesmerized
by bronzed men who serve another round.

II. Text

Eyes at dawn shot through with Vivarin—
fire and brimstone blasted through
a pair of 6 x 9 triaxials our first
drive through the South. Was it Death
riding on a Harley to our left, giving us
the finger as we fishtailed over
those Carolina hills?—Union Jacks draped
across the hood of a Tarheel's truck
at a rest stop glazed with milky trails,
glory holes instead of mile markers
ticking off those distances we had come.
Must God compete with America's
indigenous sublime?—Gideon Bibles
taking root in ditches on both sides
of the road while condoms in suburbia
erupt—clover tendrils choking off
Kentucky grass where catamites now lay
spread-eagle in the shade. Sodomy
hotter than a burning cross as dusk
draws near—*receiving in themselves*
recompense of their error which was meet.

III. Music

The first eight bars of a Mormon hymn
tattooed across his ass. The station
drifts to jazz—first summer, then winter,
geraniums ablaze in sun-glazed pots
beside a grave duller than a drag queen
trapped inside the walls of a house
papered with exotic birds, her gown
falling off her shoulders like a flag
of distress. A shotgunned taste of metal
prying open those godforsaken lips
hard at work on a redneck's anus—
that halo floating between those legs
she licked while kneeling in a cornfield
along that rural road—Milt Buckner's
locked-hand style of blues from a frantic
era at the end of bebop needing to be
calmed—voices over airwaves fading
in and out to the Tabernacle Choir
are all at the mercy of our fingertips—
the Father, Son, and Holy Ghost
smeared across the spider-cracked glass.

Last Day

Let world be more than teeth flashing in the dark.

Let me be your rotisserie Christ.

History but a pile of drowned-men's bones.

Its engine running like a well-tuned ambulance.

Two sides of a war three kilometers back.

Ready for the freight trains stiffening in our laps.

Sooner or later all frolics come to a halt.

Yet this lean-to love, *mon frère!*

With sparks no less than stars grinding overhead.

Nor'easter Forty Miles Offshore

Above the water bed, a conch's curvaceous pinks
enameled into privacy—"for the openings
of the body are all mystical openings"—
dithyrambs erupting out of drunken bacchanalias
two millennia ago slowly rubbed away
by nostalgia for the illegible—this evening's
doppler radar a tentacular cloud pinwheeling
across the screen to inspire in us erotic
dread—remnants from last season's storm caught
in that ukiyo-e print where ghostly threads
stream down on figures huddled beside a cliff—

FULL FATHOM FIVE

Sailors slumped over billiard tables
wake to threads of spider
eggs parachuting onto the lips of
dying whores, a mother's
hard-edged love aglitter like the cleaved
halves of a geode sold
on deserted streets, barflies fishing
singles from a tip bowl
as last call approaches—drunken ghosts
wreathed in smoke drowning out
electric voice-box emphysema
song—loneliness like a Coke
machine that fell on a man who shook
too hard for change those hours
after-hours—Lysol-bucket slow dance
closet-crammed the only dark
we'd score with Bermudas at our heels—
early dawn sliding down
the bell of a sax fingered by a crone
still chained to the bottom
of the sea—Louis Prima's "Angelina"
echoing in a calcified
shell walled off with soundproof foam.

Watching the Battleship Potemkin

hunt in the night for meat not fit for pigs crawling

overboard on their own four legs or give us this day

our daily borscht curry sweet favor with officers hung

from the yardarm oh call the guard the time has come

not one step forward down the hatch at dawn the news

lest we alas forget decisive blows full ahead head on

MONOLOGUE WITH THE VOID

Your face to be erased. Your file

deleted. This at century's end—

not Charing Cross Road where people

met. No Kewpie dolls. Mack trucks

hijacked while he-men stop to take

a leak. The dog days of August

where one can never drink too much!

An ocean between us. Like skin

to bone, your smile a rictus, cock

sliding up my crack somewhere in

cyberspace. Me no longer able

to sleep—unread messages from here

to what we would call a virtual

loss. New epic. Till lovers log off.

HAVING TRANSCENDED THE CARES OF THIS WORLD

He stops before a head shot framed
in a beauty-shop window. Bows

to the virus lurking underneath
his own skin. Thinks about walking

back to the Met. To the Asian wing
where holes had been left behind

by termites drilling through the torso
of an unearthed Bodhisattva—

The Expulsion

Time will erode our darkest memories
as faces of ex-lovers start to fade.
Nothing to hide, we lie beneath the trees

and linger in some surreptitious breeze
where kisses are blown to the edge of shade.
Time will erode our fondest memories

as angels descend with vials of disease
to infect the love our bodies have made.
No place to hide, we kneel before the trees

and offer prayers in vain. How to appease
the laws of nature we have disobeyed
even as time erodes, our memories

no match for the Almighty God's decrees:
All shall burn till the debt in full be paid.
Too late to hide among Edenic trees

uprooted. All of us down on our knees,
stripped of everything we own but a spade
in hand as death erodes our memories—
exhausted corpses laid beneath the trees.

SINE QUA NON

A pleasure some had said to read under that.

Such moments masking as charade.

A glimpse of groin through shower steam.

A tablespoon of honey dissolving in the glass.

En garde, Monsieur, tout de suite.

That rotten peach a sitting room for wasps.

As capillaries dilate and constrict.

More fun than pickup games some shirtless boys.

Glossy pages pearled upon by spurts.

Would call right back would not.

Pale daffodils breaking through their husks.

ARCHAIC TORSO

You would have a childhood—unembarrassed
doodles colliding into stained-glass windows
of cartoon nothingness. Your mother's garden
torn by an arctic blast. And now. And soon.
Some great erotic root splitting miles of poured
concrete—suburbs you would claim as a life
hardly lived. How quickly the self dissolves
in hearsay's acid bath. Flesh knows no future
but itself, each of us mining a secret dream
till we have tasted the deepest salt. All of us
money-starved and guru-crazed, empty pages
still trying to coax anxiety out from thirty-
something skin, ungroomed forsythia bramble
sparking electric yellow along the Jersey Pike—
hedges of it right on cue beckoning another
spring. Like runes on a Mayan stele overgrown
with vines. Or Rilke sizing up that immortal
torso just days before leaving Rodin for good.

Waking Up

If love exists, it is a dollar bill
wadded in my jeans, a stranger's
jockstrap dripping on our line
as more and more dogs disappear
from the family album each year.

A Song of Experience

Those welts she left across my skin
impressed me more than van Gogh's
roses sketched outside the asylum

at Saint-Rémy. Was it just last summer
the flames began to sink their teeth
into her flesh that tried to make itself

more at home inside the morgue's gas
jets? Memory but a febrile dream—
no calamine to soothe a child's body

breaking out in hives. Nothing to keep
that boy I was from clawing through
his own skin when the lights went out.

LITTLE ELEGY IN G MINOR

A box of Chopin nocturnes handed down
from the other side of my mother's death—
evening gowns in trash bags making a little
Golgotha of their own right in the corner
of that studio we had spent all morning
emptying out—uncandled cold chaperoned
through the sill. Lullabies all of us had
already heard while drinks kept going round
the parlor after her wake assembled now
into makeshift history—bits of tenderness
discarded down the cosmos slide, each night
a phantom limb, the hours trapezing over
that sea of anonymous faces where sidereal
glances scale up the piano's mirrored lid.

To Autumn

You walk through fields of hacked-down cornstalks.
To the distant humming of monks
                                    in hem-stained robes
who cold-press matted pulp into cheesecloth drip
on the outskirts of Dubuque
                              where you still can hear
the hours toll in that cider house stormed by wasps.

Anthem for Doomed Youth

To ensnare the ear's gregarious thrall, bemoan
this lack of faith, or attenuate those snippets
arising from crude speech. From where I sit
to where he is a possibility *(sans écriture)*
with kissing-cousin vantage points and beauty
to espy. A future to annihilate for a future
glance my way, what distances the eye must
cross to survey a stranger's flesh—jot and tittle
exegesis sequestered in a vault. What solitary
function could such futile noticings serve?—
torrential pulpit tremors surging underneath,
each manacled to tumescence as the eager jaws
unhinge. Nor rescue me from sedentary pose
where casual touch grows lethal, the hours
unable to withdraw—you both jail and officer
with a ring astride your hips, your heavenly
girth sufficient to that arsenal we exhaust.

II

Felix Culpa

Down on all fours.

The breaking of rules
the only rule.

Cut off from clear lines
of retreat.

Beguiled by excess.

By like-minded folk
enthroned

in ever tinier courts.

With Cherubim and a Flaming Sword

The bed of grass too damp where love too soon
      became historic. Heavy fossil. Feelings
ushered in where paradise had stood. How easy

to disregard well-meaning commands that lulled
      them into safety where hands touched
nothing. Or was the intellect to blame, suffused

with hostile glamour? Accusations issuing forth
      from such unruly mouths—ignorant
of the simple bliss that they had always known.

A BLESSING

She does not seem to know her husband
stops at a roadside strip club each night
   after work, nor does she know he gets
     taken for an extra twenty to some back
   room where those pussies in fishnet
panties hover just inches from his face
   night after night in some hypnotic dance.
     Nor does she know he somehow chooses
   not to touch, only to be witness to this
extremity. And every night he returns
   to the wife at home inexplicably refreshed.

THE MARRIAGE

Quite spent. Having gained
a minimal share, the focus

group moves on. New life
bursts through ever-elusive

promised lands receding
in times of fat: a bungalow

wrapped up in burnt-out
Xmas lights. Not feeding

is also a kind of feeding
that feeds on everything

we have known, our child
already two years dead.

THE ASSIGNATION

Each hour, the marriage
worsens. The heart

undresses and a child feels
exposed. You want to

say all's clear but words
continue to fail us

as waitresses pour cup after
cup of coffee and take

the empty glasses of wine
away. I too want to

take you away from here,
away from all this

chatter. Somewhere else
to warm these hands

grown cold as the evening
darkens, comes on—

THE GATES OF HELL

Easy to overlook at first,
his charm more than just
a snare between the hot

hors d'oeuvres and a glass
of Chambolle-Musigny.
Between his entrance

and the silence of that
room we found ourselves
finally in, unadorned

of those quizzical looks
and a public face freed
from inquisition, another

room between us opened
wherein we could feast
without anyone's notice.

Sturm und Drang

Cut flowers in clay vases attempting to give shape.

Cruel speech soiling the nuptial bed.

To navigate love's hostile seas.

Luminous sails all breeze to the bedside marriage hearse.

Bloodlines fit for hell-bent deities.

Forgotten in the bleached amphitheater of the skull.

This then the Agamemnon hour.

Think of nothing but the flesh all present tense.

Of honeyed birds and a cask of wine absence lassoed in.

Hic et Nunc

To speak the unspeakable in a tavern
run by fools who flaunt hard facts
we contrive to forget—a fag bashing
a lover's brains with hammer blows
followed by twenty-two sleeping pills—
moral credos but heroic daydreams
staged by affluence: *O sink hernieder,*
Nacht der Liebe. A notorious flop
that opened and closed like a diary
from Tangiers. Struck down from afar
as each of us shook with laughter—
his mum's false teeth an icon for all
too violent fare inured to fleeting joy.

Just You Wait

our mother said as the plates came
crashing down on entry-hall tile
aglitter with Waterford shards—
each of us marooned on that ocean
of willowware with nowhere else
to turn. *Just wait till your father
comes home to this!* said with a sense
of accomplishment, a tiny flag
standing straight up on our mailbox
by the curb where a neighborhood
hush continued on, preserving
a tone in us that we had somehow
always known whenever our home
began to sail out of the harbor—

Il Trittico

I.

A lyric coloratura bows down to a lion
fired in a kiln—thousands of sultry
colors the legacy left by this *fanciulla*
of the South. Not just another haute-
couture specialist, her highest notes
made us see God. Intimate. Stentorian.
Ovations her pride. Encores ever louder
in the other room till someone opened
the door. Mother's tears made her look
17. We all had to start somewhere,
even Callas—"Casta Diva" sung in G
verging on disaster. Voices are nothing
without the flesh, without the clay feet
of Nebuchadnezzar's dream—arias
bound in faded spines where dust motes
still rise up that staircase to the sun.

II.

Mother making soup out of her body—
razor blades discarded "with makeup
on her face that could not be more
beautiful." Or so my father said,
reciting from his Milton on patches
of dried sod. Drink deep at the roots—
torn treads on the highway where mobs
of ants carried off a writhing grub
in what appeared to be the audible
shape of a scream. How their voices
roared each night above our heads—
sleep's armor pulling all of us down
into the ground. Tongues entwined
in mouths that made one bell. China-
berries lodged in a child's ear canal.

III.

Heaps of pay stubs accrue in a mind
unaccounted for. My father retires
and the world seems a smaller place—
those flea-market castoffs scattered
through the house. Plimsolls. Bridoons.
No Tiger Balm. Nor ginseng root thick
enough for the loosest fist-fucked hole
aboard our ferry heading for the Cape's
scorched tip—ultraviolet vectors criss-
crossing a face grown ripe with crow's
feet leading to a high-noon gallows
squint amidst that chorus of "YMCA"
pumped out from the ship's rusty p.a.
We adjust our flies and someone says:
one less person to stand among us
in that long line leading to the grave.

Tenderness in a Dark Age

Shadows of headstones
lengthen as I burn

the photos—old lovers
wreathed in flame,

mouths still hungry
for whatever there was

to get—all of us
before an open grave

where one would survive
to bury the other.

ANNIVERSARY

Landscapes that grow flatter every year.

The monthly rent check due.

Camouflaged by smoke.

Could someone open a window in here?

A marriage in lieu of talk.

Regrets to inform.

Kept inside those angry Russian tomes.

F-Stop

She straddles a Shaker chair,
stilettos braced against
a hardwood floor. Angling in

the lens, her father kneels—
each object in the room
propped against the other.

Getting There

with a man who carries roses, a bundle of cut
stems drying in his fist. No words exchanged,
  only looks that quickly volley back and forth,
then seated side by side on this Port Authority
  bus heading for Hoboken, knees touching
when I ask, "How are them roses holding up?"
  He asks if I would like to have one, then adds,
"Something for your girlfriend." This single
  long-stemmed beauty now starting to fall apart
as I lift it up to my face, the bus first veering
  this way, that way, soon the entire length
of our thighs pressing hard against each other
  as we ride in silence the rest of the way home.

Bisexuality

His credentials? He says he did it
with a boy or two long before
his pubes set in. Says he'd
do it again were he not already
married. Says his wife completely
understands, having done it
herself with a sorority girl
before they ever met. I'm drinking
my beer as slowly as I can,
nursing it like the truth I know
will finally get told, peeling off
the labels on my Amstel Light—
first the neck, working my way
on down the front, and then
the back. This could take all night.

Noli Me Tangere

Backseats creaking with turbulent love
promise to lead to more—a cordless phone

hurled across a room full of daytime
talk-show hosts, the rabbit ears unable

to fine-tune any station. Frost licking
at the panes where curtains hung on

cast-iron rods crowned with fleur-de-lis
finials. As if a therapist were more

consequential than a kiss. Ski-masked
boys skating through town in search

of a goal. Your ass. The cars parked
along the road up to their doors in snow.

THE MARRIAGE

Always felt her voice was something foreign
as they rode bareback between tragedy
and farce—

Victorian roofline where the sky folds in.

Xmas trees discarded at roadside's edge.

Lottery balls colliding in a Plexiglas sphere
like a penny-ante gathering of glitterati.

Each act of love an injury,
an exhausted lexicon—

His number-crunching tendencies magnified
by saddle tramps pumping up their hopes.

A steep pile of monthly bills giving way
to mullioned windows offering up
their view of spinnakers bobbing in the bay—

And ever the grave nearer at hand.

Subway rats gnawing flattened scabs of gum
when he awoke to the morning-after
mud slide of her ravished looks—

Collagen injections reconstructing a love
that should have gone straight to video.

Less and less earnings value.

Diamond-cracking coal dust lining innocent lungs.

Child's play as paradigm.

For management's Pavlovian dog digging up the yard.

Wall Street's bird's-eye view no match for cash.

Or crash.

Maenads engaged in eternal pursuit.

Round and round the rim of a red-figure vase.

A torso bathed in washes of glaze ready for the kiln.

Depicted sitting on an ass.

Or Hera's throne.

Little of the original polychromy survives.

Roses in his cheeks that would make our century blush.

A face deprived of sleep limoed into dawn.

The fan base growing thin.

The doubts settling in.

Like the haunches of a wolf cloaked beside the hearth.

III

OF THEE I SING

A nation awash in Eurotrash finding itself upstaged.

Millions in bullion buried under rubble.

Disaster really cooking now.

Our ledgers neither ruled nor able to go on.

Tell me the secret under the secret.

Drunken teens lighting up.

Trapped inside an suv plastered with American flags.

ALL HALLOWS

Porch-lit jack-o'-lanterns oozing wax
as children march to the local mall
with empty pillow sacks. The doorbell

rings. No one answering it. Nothing
through gauze curtains to be seen
but a clawed-up love seat left behind.

in the wake of a love gone wrong. Intentions

nothing more than a parlor game as the storm
came on. Where a pool of curbside antifreeze

cast its luminous shroud as children writing

in chalk were suddenly called in—faint Muzak
of a passing ice-cream truck catching them

off guard. The times you could almost taste

such cool against your lips but never given
the chance—the prize in the gumball machine

always *for someone else.* Perhaps it was best

to go without in that neighborhood ravaged
by age, your body as yet immune to groans

in the dark for which there were no remedies.

From Sea to Shining Sea

I. Red

Bonnie Raitt bootlegs blasting blues
and slide guitar while Serb elections

cratered. How many hits went platinum
overnight while sanctions on gallons

of rationed gas left correspondents
incommunicado? (Clinton and Bush

already a media blitz, ringside seats
for the Tyson fights a pay-per-view

extravaganza.) So what if poetry
burns itself into the ground—empire

of paper whose only prayer is ash
wiped across the forehead of a corpse

great with child—a bridge festooned
with tires on the brink of collapse.

II. White

Crack-head b-ball junkies in jail
or dead. Cabrini Green ponying up

for politicians—no Contract
with America more promising than

a low-level service job. Or a bite
of sound. What all those homeboys want

are "props" and "burners," dribbling
out of that ghetto with gold caps

on their teeth. Fuck the nine-to-five.
Pass those bottle caps cooked

with a match—needle stuck in the neck
of a woman giving head as a child

clings to her back, still sucking
on a pacifier—old enough to speak.

III. Blue

A "non-reactive" test. We would lie
on a mound of pansies behind the park

and fondle ourselves in that torpid air
where glimpses of rising balloons

filled us with desire. (My anus yet
unentered, no thought of your member

tearing through my body—the sound
of lambskin breaking as stray dogs

roamed the neighborhood, digging up
the gardens.) Innocence means nothing

to us now. We raise the blinds, living
from test to test, trying not to feel

lucky as we breathe this morning air
now pouring in through a torn screen.

At County General

Left to slowly roast in his own artistic fat.

Locked inside a Cibachrome square.

Christian tracts papered over a tearoom door.

Taking root inside a stranger's eager throat.

Going down on virgin groin.

Fragrances that won't wash off plaguing us.

Our smiles sailing past all the local stops.

Shoved down subway stairs.

A nest of forty stitches with eyes bruised shut.

As voices pool and swell inside his inner ear.

Songs We Know but Cannot Sing

Has-been bands fueling our angst where lust
grows ripe in a gypsy's womb. Birth me!
cries the troll, make me new again so that I

might live another hour inside my own skin.
Drowsed in a haze of poppers, we cruise
the tiled corridors of some abandoned gym

where youth has just up and gone—festering
sores on a stranger's cock but the tiniest
of mouths still crying out their deepest song.

No Worse Off Than a Houseboy Unemployed

The questions of august heaven left
to hair-splitting arguments in a beat-up
copy of the *Analects* for two bits
dropped in a tackle-box slot at the local
library sale. Where boys have gone
to spy *The Joy of Sex* among cold stacks
longing for touch. For the mantic arts
ensconced in huts barbed off by private-
property signs. Bored of cruising
the Campo Santo de Las Cruces. Sick
of man-sized portions of chorizo
enchiladas riding shotgun on their way
out of town, action in the "curious-
but-not-gay" menu option gone wrong
again on that 1-900 bulletin board
hanging in what's left of the Wild West—

TARGET

Sun-bleached forelock poking out of a backwards
baseball cap. And it's spring again—jeans torn

above both knees, the crotch mended with a patch.
This morning's sun lighting up the length of it

from here to where you are, a bathrobe coiled
around your feet. Had wanted to say. Had loved

the place. The spot quote: *staging the appearance*
as disappearance. It's spring again—a squadron

of tornadoes touching down near Disney World, all
the world "Disneyfied," or so you said slumming

across Times Square that summer before the sex
stores closed—El Niño up against the West Coast.

Bleecker Street

Desire mapping stringencies across a stranger's chest
marked by razor burns, waistbands of designer briefs
hinting at the bulge I seek (half-eaten bagel tossed back
and forth between two thugs who loiter at a subway
stop)—the anorexic tits of a sylphlike nymph pressed
under Plexiglas. To be sandwiched like that—flat
images filling up rush-hour space where commuters wait.
Nothing to lend some depth to this scene, nothing
upright as the rails snake under the city—a drag queen
singing on a train leaving town. If she is not lovely,
then a lemon has no scent, no sunlight at its center,
the night no match for stiletto struts in gold lamé—
hubris poised in five-inch heels braving the sewer grates.

IN HOT PURSUIT

across the Passaic's asphalt drawbridge into the heart of Kearny—
my cheeks flushed with wine—you the muse I did not choose
dragging danger down in chains across the hangdog face of me

as I followed you upriver, wanting you to cleanse me like a sari
pulled through a virgin's wedding band—why else would I cruise
across the Passaic's asphalt drawbridge into the heart of Kearny

still hot on your brand-new tail?—yes, you—my spanking Jersey
princess with a papa's pocketbook good for nothing but booze
and chains of smoke you'll drag across the hangdog face of me

until I cry myself to sleep in the priest's confessional, unworthy
of your whorish looks and your windows down blasting blues
across the Passaic's asphalt drawbridge into the heart of Kearny

with a fifth of Maker's Mark sloshing in your lap more empty
than the gas was ever gonna get when I got through—win or lose—
love but a daisy chain dragged across the hangdog face of me

until crush felt more like crash upside another tab of Ecstasy
hurled overboard with seat belts coming loose and pairs of shoes
spilled across Passaic asphalt straight into the heart of Kearny
where danger dragged its tread across the hangdog face of me.

A CROWN

thrown down. An empty throne
at a loss for minion—heart's

disquiet pooling at the edge
of thought. No visible ruins

to detect just now as kingdoms
drift into provinces of sleep

with fortitude aplenty sallying
forth across such lyrical atoll.

La Divina

Astrological consultations giving birth to a boy.

Never had a childhood only a mask.

Even in a mirror the face could not be seen.

Even the least could teach her what she could not do.

"The mind must work not too much also."

Of hair-raising stature.

Not just another jet-set *coup de foudre.*

The priestess and the woman wrestling in a single mind.

Behind the mask another mask.

Invisible strings suspended by a floating cross.

"More than my best I cannot promise."

More man than woman.

More than a woman flattered by a ruffian's utter charm.

A victim of bad press.

Fallout not routine but event itself.

Left to fend for herself on such tenterhooks.

Such hopes to sing again.

A colossal voice ever in decline.

Without applause without rapport simply left without.

Visiting My Mother's Grave

Something's kept me away, perhaps
an all too familiar voice laced with
paranoia streaming through a phone

unhooked from its cradle, dangling
in that empty room. Hanging up
not an option. Her ashes in an urn

for the third straight year and now
I wonder how it was I never could
get through to her. Yet here I am.

ROMANCE

Just as I finished my second glass
of port, anticipating the passion-

fruit soufflé crowned with a cloud
of crème fraîche—my face & chest

broke out in hives. You grabbed
my hand, & I said don't worry, it's

only Mother trying to get through—

Woman with Dog, 1917

Meaty flowers plastered to a stuffed
crimson chair, her folded elbows
propped on a canine's jackaled spine—
the lapdog's triangular head at rest
facing us like an enormous blackened
sex. It made its way to the Midwest
nonetheless—a gift from Owen &
Leone Elliot who could spot a fair
Soutine. Imagine them looking at this
thing each night in their farmhouse
along the edge of the Iowa River
with a meat-and-potatoes mouthful
of corn right off the cob. No wonder
they had no choice but to give it up.

Wake Me Up When the Real Opera Begins

More tease than ruse our intentions were. Naked
to the word and our bedside antics so avant-garde.

The screen kiss did us in. And you who left me
stripped of feeling, armored as you were against

amour with all its comely trappings from an age
that had outgrown itself. Come ye hither sporting

plumes and bells about the ankles? Such parades
in whorish silks when sackcloth most becomes us.

LIKE AN EMPEROR GORED BY A PAPAL BULL

To distance oneself
   from the easel, the table, the example
      set by others long since dead
         who shared a studio on the Rue Pigalle

in the ninth arrondissement—
   a screen depicting women in a garden
      with pigment unto pleasure
         rejected by the Salon—the public's fickle

pocketbooks unclasped
   like an era, a century of discord
      offset by pictorial
         extravagance—sons who once had studied law

at their father's behest
   sworn into a cult of moonlit chinoiserie—
      evolving interests made more
         manifest on the mind's frayed tapestry

between heirloom
   and estate, twilight and croquet, the leisure
      class framed by the parlor's strict
         geometry, its preassembled forms sprinkled

through a catalog
   wind torn by the rain—pages cured and stained
      in that unrelenting sun—
         an *idée fixe* centering the altarpiece

beneath memory's
   gilded apse, the verbal tesserae of speech
      reverberating through that
         cavernous dark as host to a congregation

of one—whore and maiden
    caught in a full-scale study of modest restraint
        sans clientele parading
            before a cloudburst of disease and delight—

appetite's voracious
    jaws rusting shut on what?—a lexicon ending
        with a final gasp unheard
            by those who gather around an open grave

in the name of love?—
    of effulgent floral elegance so pungent
        in its sense of timely doom,
            this occasion magnified not in marble

dust freely falling
    from that chisel gripped in a child's rosy hands
        but in a world perfumed
            by the foulness of our own breath extending

only so far—the sieve
    of humanitas enclosing us in a tomb,
        an open-air replica
            fit for an audience not of our making

nor of our wanting—
    the future personified as a faceless
        crowd ever inching towards
            the promontory from which ambition leapt

spread-eagle into
    the void—an attempt to embrace the unmet
        adulation that strips us
            of our flesh and all of its attendant woes—

Sally Keith, *Dwelling Song*
Maurice Kilwein Guevara, *Postmortem*
Joanna Klink, *They Are Sleeping*
Caroline Knox, *To Newfoundland*
Steve Kronen, *Empirical Evidence*
Patrick Lawler, *A Drowning Man Is Never Tall Enough*
Sydney Lea, *No Sign*
Jeanne Lebow, *The Outlaw James Copeland and the Champion-Belted Empress*
Phillis Levin, *Temples and Fields*
Timothy Liu, *Of Thee I Sing*
Rachel Loden, *Hotel Imperium*
Gary Margolis, *Falling Awake*
Tod Marshall, *Dare Say*
Joshua McKinney, *Saunter*
Mark McMorris, *The Black Reeds*
Mark McMorris, *The Blaze of the Poui*
Laura Mullen, *After I Was Dead*
Jacqueline Osherow, *Conversations with Survivors*
Jacqueline Osherow, *Looking for Angels in New York*
Tracy Philpot, *Incorrect Distances*
Paisley Rekdal, *A Crash of Rhinos*
Donald Revell, *The Gaza of Winter*
Andy Robbins, *The Very Thought of You*
Martha Ronk, *Desire in L.A.*
Martha Ronk, *Eyetrouble*
Tessa Rumsey, *Assembling the Shepherd*
Peter Sacks, *O Wheel*
Aleda Shirley, *Chinese Architecture*
Pamela Stewart, *The Red Window*
Susan Stewart, *The Hive*
Donna Stonecipher, *The Reservoir*
Terese Svoboda, *All Aberration*
Terese Svoboda, *Mere Mortals*
Sam Truitt, *Vertical Elegies 5: The Section*
Lee Upton, *Approximate Darling*